Voices Writ in Sand

Voices Writ in Sand

Dramatic Monologues and Other Poems

by
Jeffrey DeLotto

LAMAR UNIVERSITY PRESS

ISBN: 978-0-9852552-3-7
Library of Congress Control Number: 2012944336

Book Design: Arwin Burkett
Manufactured in the United States of America

Lamar University Press
Beaumont, Texas

To Dudley, who helped me learn to listen

As the poet John Keats was dying of tuberculosis at the age of twenty-five, thinking he had hardly been noticed, he asked that he should be described on his grave as one "whose name was writ in water." But voices dwell, longer than we ourselves sometimes know, and for me the dramatic monologue often affords voices a habitation and a name.

The voices on the following pages have been heard, sometimes face to face, sometimes in the mind's eye, sometimes from those we might call ordinary folk, but when we listen, we know there are no ordinary folk but only remarkable selves seldom heard. So listen, read these aloud, hear with me our voices, these persons writ in the sand of a sounding shore.

Acknowledgments

I am grateful to the following for their publication of individual poems in previous versions:

"A Confederate on the Square, Columbia, Tennessee," *descant: Lone Star 2000*

"A Memory among the Islands," *RiverSedge* 8:1 (Fall 1993)

"A Moneychanger outside the Temple," *Days of a Chameleon: Collected Poems*

"A Morning Start, Sage Creek Ranch," *New Texas 2001*

"A Stripper's Surgery, Dallas," *New Texas 2000*

"A Voice from the Chapel, Mission San Antonio de Valero," *Connecticut River Review*

"An Unfortunate Encounter with a Lady," *Langdon Review of the Arts in Texas*(2009)

"Iliana, In Southern Bulgaria," *Alacran: A Literary Review* 9 (November 1996)

"In the Parish Churchyard, Westbury-on-Trym," *CCTE Studies* (1992)

"Islamorada," *RiverSedge* 6:2 (Spring 1992)

"Geronimo, Fort Pickens, Pensacola Bay, Florida, July, 1887," *SouthLit.com* (June 2006)

"Gloucester Cathedral," *Terrapin: A Literary Review* 8 (November 1995)

"Mio-Qua-Coo-Na-Caw (Red Pole), Village Chief, Shawnee Nation," *Voices at the Door*

"Moncrief Radiation Center," *A Book of the Year 1991*, Poetry Society of Texas

"Moving the Herd, he Busenitz Place, Wyoming," *CCTE Studies* (September2007)

"On Finding a Grey Fox," *Days of a Chameleon: Collected Poems*

"On Seeing a Snakeskin Shed in Hurd Cemetery," *Seams: The Cultural Arts Journal* (1990)

"On Shaving, St. Joseph Peninsula, Florida," *New Texas: A Journal of Literature and Culture*

"On the Point, Plantation Key, Florida," *Alura Quarterly* (Summer 1991)

"Rooster Bridge, Demopolis, Alabama, 1919," *Horny Toad* (November 1993)

"Route 35, Texas Gulf Coast," *Days of a Chameleon*

"Ruined Vessels," *RiverSedge* 6:2 (Spring 1992)

"St. Archangel Cemetery, Plovdiv, Bulgaria," *Preying Mantis* (November 1994)

"The Fourth Sunday of Easter," *Voices at the Door*

"The Suq at Irbid, Jordan, 1981," *Aura Literary/Arts Review* 26 (Spring/Summer 1989)

"The Whistle Buoy," *The Anthology of New England Writers 1997*

"The Wilderness, Near Spotsylvania Courthouse, Spring, 1864," *Voices at the Door*

"Two Hawks Kindles a Morning Fire," *Langdon Review of the Arts in Texas* 6 (2009)

"Waiting, Morongu, Tanzania," *New Texas '99*

Contents

Shades

Singularities

Soldiers

Simplicities

Signs

Shades

Geronimo

Fort Pickens, Pensacola Bay, Florida

July, 1887

I remember where I began

But not why I am here.

I remember the black stone open wounds of the earth,

Sharp as skinners' knives over days of setting suns,

Stone shining when broken like water, chipped into

Points light enough to find the smallest bird—

But I do not know these red clay bricks they

Have me carry, or this great salt water that surrounds

Me here—I know the sun when he is angry as fire

And sucks dry the grass and leaves and every living

Thing, and when he glows so bright and distant that

The frost does not dry until midday. But I do not know

This face of his that squeezes oily sweat from our

Bodies, poisonous sweat that brings the fever, as

If we were rotting antelope carcasses after a rain.

And I who was bred and lived and fought and

Loved in land so dry and hard no whites could

Live in, I and my spirit are shrinking here of sweat

And sickness my own sad land could not support.

And we suck the living meat from sea rocks, and

Net the stupid fish many fingers full, fish the kin

Of snakes, with no skill or stealth or courage—
I may as well be a Hopi here.

I see you, Mangas Coloradas, long gone but
Striding through the deep smoke of the cannon
Here as they practice firing out over the bay, I
Long to meet Juana and Alope and my daughters,
Wandering lost spirits in the Mexican Sierras,
But I cannot die. What great punishment that I
Who cannot die from a bullet, thought a powerful
Medicine once, now an abiding curse, I who cannot
Be hanged are so hung upon, a scarecrow of my
Time, my clothes and pots and utensils, all Pinda-
Lick-O-Ye made and pressed upon, even my name
Goyahkla, "one who yawns" soaked into the sand
Like spilled blood, become "Geronimo," from the
Mouths of the Mexicans I will always kill. And the
Words of Miles, "The worst Indian that ever lived"
Hang about my neck like a Navajo amulet.

Yesterday a mule harnessed to a heavy wagon
Stepped into soft sand between two pine roots
And broke his leg with a sound like an old pinon
Branch, and Corporal Sanders shot him before our
Evening meal behind the southern dunes and we
Carried shovels and buried—*buried*—that rich

2

Meat and went in to share barreled beef with beans
And corn pone, *buried*, and I could still taste the
Charred haunch we pulled from the flames, setting
The shack of those settlers alight up on the Gila—
Oh, tell me, tell me, Mangas, why I do not die. I
Am not of this land and sea, nor they me, and I carry
Cut trees and feed and sleep and am stabled at night
As god dogs are. Oh, they try, as children spoil dogs
Or dress up dolls, giving us shelter and woven clothes
Enough, even letting us dance for the corn, but always
The steamer comes and brings the grinning faces,
Women and children and soft old men, curling their
Lips in disgust or dismay or pulling them back from
Thick teeth like donkeys braying at the scent of a
Mare—at the sight of my wives cracking lice, or
Naiche, son of Cochise, calling upon Usen to carry
His spirit deep into the pine-choked canyons where
The Chiricahua hunted deer before this day.

I look out over the sometimes still waters of the Bay,
To where She-gha lay, her spirit clutching the grass
Like a ground mist, and hear our children laugh and
Play amongst the barrels and stacked shot, behind the
Chiseled stone and iron gates, laughing and singing,
And wonder when, *when*, I should die, and know
That I hear no echoes in the wind.

A Morning Start,

Sage Creek Ranch

We swung open the ringing gate across the road,
Looking onto a green-swathed meadow between
A levee on the Little Missouri and an outcropping
Of Bentonite and flint, waded into drenched dawn
Grass and shook buckets rattling with oats, calling,
"Here, Spot—C'mon here Susie Q, Roanie Baloney,
B.J., Beeg, here boy," rope halters draped around
Our necks, until Sue and then Spot, and then the
Whole remuda of a dozen horses streamed through
The gate toward the corral.

Picking our four and four more, too, for the afternoon,
We turned the rest back into the mist that still hung
In patches ankle-deep in the hollows.

And as we brushed our mounts, their muscles quivering
Under the curry bristles, bank upon bank of scents rolled
Through the barn, first old hay and the delicate nut-like
Toast of oats poured into shallow troughs, scrabbled
Up by massaging velvet lips, followed by the rhythmical
Crunch of powerful teeth busying the horses as we brushed.
Soon there followed the dropping of dung, steaming in strong-
Scented piles, bright green as fresh pesto, the path so clear

And clean from pasture grass to tight belly to slowly closing
Sphincter ring, the broad aluminum shovel tossing it out
Onto the pile to lard the garden loam for finger-thick
Asparagus to thrust through, Freudian green and strong.
Next the blankets, upended since last their use had
Wet them on a ride, were balanced on the broad
Brushed backs, the sweat wool smell pushed aside
By that of harness leather and oily soap as saddles
Were swung up into place, lifted, twisted, and settled
Again, the cinch straps and belly bands tightened.

We led the horses, Sue, Spot, B.J., and Roany, out
Into the chill sunlight, tightened cinches, slapped the
Older mare Sue trying to swell her stomach for a
Slacker ride, and swung up, heading down the road's
Shoulder, for the Red House Pasture and some thirty
Pairs of heifers and calves to gather by noon.
And this the start of each day.

A Trinity Flood

Fort Worth, Texas

May, 1876

We were digging clams down in the Trinity River
Bottom just north of Ayres' place, half a mile east
Of Sycamore Creek, had us a couple dozen, my
Sister Iola and me, even busted two open on a rock,
The hand-sized shells thick with mother of pearl,
The meat big as a chicken egg, we chewed and
Swallowed the muscle and other guts, the first
Fresh meat we'd had since Uncle Joe brought us
That calf one of his heifers dropped in April dead.

The morning was still and cook-pan hot off the
Mud and sand of the riverbed, two bleached
White buffalo skulls staring from the southern
Cut bank, washed down no doubt from a spilled
Wagonload north of town, and we hadn't paid
Any mind to the empty blue sky until a rattle
Of cottonwood leaves told of a breeze. The jack
Oaks down to high water line, their thick roots
Reaching out of the sand like down turned fingers,
Kept us from seeing, but once up on the higher
Ground, dragging our croaker sacks through thorn
And low-draped mustang grapes, we saw the north

And west horizon frowned up thick as smoke with
Storm clouds, a cool breeze swept our sweat-pointed
Hair off our brows and half-way home, the clear
Robin's egg sky not yet gone from the south,
It started to come down.

Eight days it rained, eight days and eight nights,
Almost straight through it came down, more than
Just a rain but like a being, an old beast crouching
Over us, sometimes a sprinkle, sometimes a drum-
Roll roar so hard and loud the shingles sounded like
They'd bounce off the roof....and she came out of her
Steep cut banks without hesitation, like milk welling
Out of a bottle filled by a distracted hand, like milk
Washing out almost oily onto a table, spreading past
Trees, around houses, over streets, picking up the
Dust and straw and forgotten tins and sacks, rising,
Heavy like spilled milk, like that thick brown milk
Grandmama sometimes made me on Saturdays after
Papa went out to harness the team, with bitter old coffee
From the stove and some sticky blackstrap, but I swear
I will never savor such stuff again.

A day after the rain blew by, that river moved over our
Town, more than two miles flooded out past Richland,
That dirty water moved sometimes more like a bank

Of cloud than something to loathe, until you saw the

Cows and pigs and more come bobbing by, all bloated

Out, hooves poking up like overturned table legs, until

The water crept back, leaving roads long, shiny smears,

Like tracks of mucus down some sick child's lip—

And I heard more than one man ask, not the last time

In coming days, what in hell were we doing here.

But after day nine and the sun shown down bright,

Clear, our world washed and clean, we all hung our

Clothes and linen and mattresses out on fences to dry.

After another three days the river dropped back down

Into her banks and we started seeing them, the animals

And the caught folks. Already we had some laid out,

From their houses, found in their haylofts, old Ephraim

Humphrey, Frank Forney, Colonel Henry Granger, and

Put them in the ground quick in the sticky heat, shovels

Sticking on every swing in the muck, the soaked shrouds.

But those others down closer to the Trinity, caught

In trees, one man's leg trapped beneath his wagon seat,

The whole rig bogged half-way up the bank, just hanging

There in the bright sun after the water fell back, the broken

Singletree wedged in the mud, swollen, Lord Jesus, and

The flies...and then what we found, Billy Spurlock and

I, found caught up an old rock wash where all those big

Old limestone snail shells, ribbed and an easy foot across

Kept us thinking about this book by some man named
Linnaeus Colonel Smith loaned me....I just caught a spot
Of red, thought it a cardinal I did, until the blue-white
Dimpled arm told me what she was, maybe washed and
Rolled downstream from some house in Hell's Half Acre
We had heard about, by the look of her scarlet dress and
Stockinged foot, we never did know, but me and Billy,
Before we told a soul, pulled her out, I swear we feared
She'd come apart, and her red dress and underclothes
All twisted up around her waist, and her legs like fresh
Dressed hams fell open, and we stared and stared, looked
At each other and stared again at...the woman of her,
The mystery, the way it was all inside, and we couldn't
See, and we were all outside, all on the outside, always.
We fixed her back, swore secrecy and found our folks
And put her up there outside Ayres' Cemetery with so
Many others, Mama saying Mama's sure that woman
Is in a better place, but I kept quiet.

Now, as we roll and steam into the twentieth century,
My practice, Evangeline, the children doing well, Billy
Down in Austin and us with a new courthouse and college
And rail yards and all, everyone is saying that a golden
Day is upon us, but I see that old Trinity snaking down
There in the clay, I recall a lost soul who showed herself
To a stranger, and I am not so sure.

Ruined Vessels

Tucked into a fold of the Mendip hills

A stone barn stands, the molded slates

Fallen in from the burden of a farm's fate,

Releasing my mind to dream and to fill

The void with ruddy-cheeked faces still

Plump and fat with rich cream and cakes,

The father heated with ale, his stubborn hate

Working the stony soil, the callused mother still

Sweeping the gritty stoop; always the sheep,

Button-eyed, graze on a placket of green -

Only the geese, nasal and offended, marching.

Ruined buildings do that: let one leap

To another time, unallayed, long unseen,

And fill shells ready for dreams and imaginings.

Two Hawks Kindles a Morning Fire

Natchitoches Confederacy, ca. 1810

Aren't you up early, little tat'iti?

Come sit while I start my fire for tea.

What do I do? I wrap my hand in doeskin,

Holding my steel so—this foreign flint has

Cut my fingers too many times, but this kindling wool and

Flint is not the moss your mother arranges, and you note my steel,

The ends curled? Long seasons past I was given this tool

By an old man from another people far north of here....But

This is a story for another day. Yes, the dried tree moss they

Use works well, but from where did it come? Ah, the sparks

I struck have brought life to my little kindle here. Hand me

Those small sticks behind you....The moss that hangs all

About us here—when first our people came to this place,

There and water, swamp, everywhere as it is now, but the

Trees growing out of the mud were bare, and our people of

The Caddo grew and planted our corn and squash and peppers,

Wove and bundled our lodges as we do today, and took deer

And bear as we pleased.

One day a man and his son came in a dugout shaped as we had

Never seen—Caloosa, they said, on a journey of the spirit, and

Showed us beautiful shells and a stick-thrown spear that was

Fast and true—they were a wondrous pair—and as they spoke,

11

The son, called Osceokla, looked deeply into the spirit of Dark
Moon, a tinuti maiden just blooded, her black shining hair falling
On either side, through her deep black eyes, his spirit reached,
And sat by her fire until they could not be apart. No, sihnuti,
He was not a skin-walker, as your mother warns you of, but
Only a youth feeling the love of a woman for the first time, as
She, lost in each other's hearts....You will not understand for
A long time, but listen—Locksawee, the elder Caloosa, saw
His son slipping from his grasp, and Dark Moon's father saw,
Too, the two Caloosa with their journey not complete; Tichtow
Forbade his daughter to sit in the lodge when Osceokla sat with
His father; Locksawee, saw, too, the journey might end here,
Before the destined time, the two elders agreeing. And the two
Caloosa poled away on the morning of the next day, soon lost
In the mist that hung like the smoke of a memory over the track
Between the cypress trees, the hard light of day soon burning
Away any trace of where the men had gone, in all but the eyes
Of Dark Moon, whose thick lashes were stroked together into
Points by the slow tears of grief, not with sound of wailing or
Sigh but with the slow squeeze of deepening loss.
And day spun into day and into night, Dark Moon's bowl of corn
Meal and bright peppers untouched, joints of venison or even soft
Catfish unbroken in her lap, her long blue-black hair hanging down
Her cheeks unbraided and unbrushed.

Until one summer day, Dark Moon, her strength failing, her heart
Knowing Osceokla would never return, wound her way through

Thicket and brush, past blackberry and clutching thorn, deeper into
The swamp, wading through sloughs and past chuckling creeks,
Deeper into the cypress stands than ever she had known her people
To tread before. And there she saw a cypress tree taller than all
The others, on a mound of mossed soil, the knees of the old tree
Rising up all around like the thick fingers of the yearning dead.
She propped a fallen trunk onto the bole and pulled herself onto
The lowest branch and began to reach up and climb, step and pull,
Until the surrounding trees fell away and the clean untouched breeze
Swept her face and lifted her tangled hair.

And there she took three long sinews from her brightly beaded
Pouch adorned with a glossy pink bit of shell Osceokla had given
Her. Twisting the sinews together she tied the cord around the one
Thick branch remaining, the other around her smooth throat, and
Spreading wide her empty fingers stepped off into the keening air.
And all that season Dark Moon's body swayed in the moving wind
And slowly dried, untouched by bird or furry hand, her black doeskin
Shift hardened in the broken sun, her long blue-black hair caught
And lifted, turned as the season passed, lost its gloss and grew from
Blue to dull black and then to moldy grey, the wind lifting her
Heavy tresses, until a long storm swept in out of the south, turning
Slowly as the water turns in my tea here. And the powerful winds
Pulled at Dark Moon's corn-husk form from side to side until her
Hair was drawn from the leathered skull, was pulled and caught,
Caught and drawn from tree to tree, from where the sun comes up

13

To where it goes down—her hair grey and swollen with grief drapes
Still from our branches. Such moss cannot kindle my fire, though
Many use it to. Yes, children, that is why the moss in the trees
Sometimes makes you sad.

Here, now, that happened long ago. Taste these berries I dried
Into sweetened spots for my tea.

The Whistle Buoy

A blocked fuel line, a fallen breeze, and
I was behind, trying to make Dauphin Island
And an anchorage across a long and open stretch
Of shoaling sound, but down the sun dropped,
A luminous gold, a knowledge and an eye,
Before I made the shore.

Night drew its cloak tight around my shoulders,
Moonless, a glittering shower of stars overhead,
But a low mist and a hard chop, an old chart
Kept comfort out of reach, as I longed to
Drop the hook and rest.

Out of the deep mystery of the dark,
Under the sound of wind and waves
Was carried the low and calm hoooot
Of the whistle buoy, a long pause, and again
The sad refrain telling of wellhead or wreck,
The hoooot blowing slow and passionless
Out of the dense fabric of the dark,
Like some drowned corpse playing a bone flute,
The fleshless fingers touching the holes,
The ghost of a sailor blowing the notes,
Calling for company under the waves,

Calling me to my grave,

And I was afraid.

A Karankawa

Near Garcitas Creek, Matagorda Bay
October, 1684

Have some tea, Monsieur LeBon, is that how
You say it? Boiled from that Yaupon holly at
The edge of the sand, the tea will make you strong
Again; use this bowl with the handle I found near
Your staying place. Here, I will hold it for you,
Your hands are of course bound very tight with
The Yucca fiber, not as smooth as your boat's
Rope but good enough for us poor Karankawa.
Oh, don't lift your eyes to the sky, the tears, like
A welcoming Caddo there, but the pain will pass,
And we have much to share, you and I, and I
Grow hungry—yes, LeBon, if eyes could pierce,
I would be full of holes and I would now die,
But I will not, nor will you. That last slice I took,
From your lower back, just a hand's length piece,
The width and depth of the middle finger I lost
To the snapping jaws of that wild pig four seasons
Past, you faced it like a man, until you saw it spit
And crackle over the fire, until my first slow bite,
Sprinkled with a pinch of salt from the drying stone,
Though a man's flesh does not need much added salt,
So well greased and spiced we already are…and now

You understand I will consume your spirit piece
By piece until you exist only in me. Come, sit up,
The sun is very tall, all those coverings you wear
Make you sweat so, and your skin so bright, no
Tattoos to show who you are, but I will change all
That today, eh? But let me pull off one of those
Long leather cases you have on our feet—pah!—
How they stink, but the big toe, LeBon, that big,
Soft fat toe, how it will pop and sizzle—I see I
Must wrap the legs together, so, along this trunk
Of driftwood before you will let me have it, and
This knife you brought us, so bright and shiny,
Remember? But perhaps an arm is better, up near
The last joint, where you can see the swiftness of
My knife, and I don't wish you to faint away into
A world of ignorance—a man should be aware of
Himself and where he is going...See? You felt
Just a chill, like brushing against a frosty branch,
And then the sting as the edge made its way through
The skin, and so sharp, just a handful of bright red
Beads of blood, the flap still held closed, and, here,
LeBon, look into my eyes, and—see? You did not
Guess the second cut so soon—Stay with me a short
Span of day longer, breaking man, so that I might hold
Your essence like an opened oyster and slide it down
My upturned throat....Uh, he is gone for now, into
That forced sleep of fear.

LeBon and I have time until he wakes again, and here
Growing along this stream are fine straight canes for
Arrow shafts to replace those I lost in that beautiful
Snook that swam off a day ago near the sandspit's tip,
Oh, what food that fish would have been for all my
Family. But I look at this piece of bleeding man and
Have to wonder what drove him here, and will I feel
That pull, and how many more will we share into our
Bodies until our spirits become theirs?

Waiting

Morongu, Tanzania

Out by the gate to the park

At Kilimanjaro, so well they wait,

The men and boys, to be porters, or cooks,

Or guides, or they just simply wait, easy,

So skilled at that, on the bright grass,

And under towering eucalyptus trees shedding

Bark like sloppy snakes, wait near the wire

Fence, where green-clad guards casually cradle

Kalashnikovs shiny with handling rather than

Use--they wait, and chat with friends, in

Swahili heavy with throated vowels, they wait

In shade and sun, for something, or nothing

At all, their heads in a row looking like dots,

Periods, a human ellipsis, waiting for

Completion....

The Suq at Irbid

Fall, 1981

I.

A magical meld of east and west, north and south,

Anachronisms of winding streets, donkeys and sheep,

Plumed and painted taxis, braying lorries

Welling from the suqs, the storied ones

In Damascus and Timbuktu and Dar es Salaam

In Luxor, Baghdad and dusty Cairo;

The provincial at Oom Qais, Ma'an, and Soof,

And here in Irbid, bride of the north—

Irbid, hid between the Jordan's breeding banks

And the folded Syrian plains, where on a clear day

You see the snows of Old Mount Nebo north,

And east the rough brown sand of Arabia,

And I, an ajnabi, an Engleesi, went to

The suq on Thursday, Muslim market day,

And was swept away in the turgid stream.

II.

Past wads of dried yoghurt the size of a child's fist,

Necklace strings of okra, sacks of broad beans,

The scorched bundles of brush holding chick-pea pods

Tied with gingham rags, thrust at me by boys,

Spilled burlap bags of charcoaled wood

From the hills owned by no man,

21

Thumb-sized eggplants, tough cauliflower, onions

All dried and thick from the desert heat;

Bolts of brown British wool for winter robes

And dishdashes, with matching Western coats

Summer galibayyehs made in China--Golden Cock brand,

Golden Cock brand shoe polish, sewing machines,

Switch-blades, pipe wrenches, socks,

And alarm clocks you hear ticking two rooms away,

Golden cock needles and thread and cookies

And canned walnuts and plump white asparagus;

Beef frozen in Bulgaria, Australian mutton and mince,

Small frozen chickens, Brazilian, dark and tough,

Gold liter-tins of ghee and lard from Holland

Libyan olive oil freely given, sold cheap,

Austrian full-cream powdered milk, tinned jam,

And candy, candy bars and pieces, candied almonds

Mints, chocolate from Italy, France, England,

Turkish delight, candied apricots, and kilo

Bricks of figs, Iraqi Stallion Brand dates,

Pistachios, and the acrid-sweet aroma,

Mouth-filling, of dark roast African coffee

Toasted in drums with Cardamom.

III.

And over the horns and hawkers' cries,

Through thick smells of sweets and spice,

22

Echoing down the mazing streets and walks

of stone and concrete shops, of stands and carts,

The sound snaking out from high, horned speakers

Making most words tin and hollow and dead,

Alive the sound, reaching out from minarets,

Aaaawuoooyiiaaullah ak-barrr, love and power,

Winding down into a call to prayer,

And again, Aaaaawuoooyiiaayllah ak-barrr,

The call, the recognition, the gratitude,

Allah akbar—God is great—no God but Allah,

And Muhammed is his Prophet.

Shops shut up their doors,

Pulled down hinged steel shutters,

Some shopkeepers or stall hawkers,

Moved forward to curb or threshold's edge,

Sleeves rolled past the elbow, feet sandaled

Trousers rolled to the knee, bright pink

Or green plastic pitchers sloshing in hand,

And washed hands and arms, feet and ankles,

And devout rapt and serious faces,

The water running clean and free over stone;

The men move to the backs of their shops

Or to the tarpaulin's edge, bowed, humbled,

Portals of the soul cleansed, kneel and prostrate

Their bodies, their minds and hearts

To the God of the Prophet,

To the God of their aging world,

And are made secure, and belong.

IV.

Black-wrapped Bedouin women poke

Through scarred tomatoes, spotted apples

And oranges, broken carrots and roots,

Or looking for a chicken to consecrate and slit,

Haggling over cucumbers and glossy shoes,

The women's burgundy neck-cloths wagging,

Wild and bright pink gypsy-scarves encased

Leather faces flashing gold teeth like gamblers,

These old Bedouins yelling, gesturing,

Jostling on past crates and jerry cans.

The men swaggering ahead, carrying only the beads,

Clicking the prayer beads idly in one hand,

Hawk-faces hard and pitiless as olive wood,

The brigands of the wadis, of the old ways,

Still slipping high-piled Mercedes lorries

Packed with American cigarettes, Levis,

And perfume, and people, too, uprooted

Lives looking for richer soil, for papers,

For peace—the pirates dance this contraband

Over the mine fields, over frontiers

Drawn on some soiled colonial's map,

The trucks rocking and groaning on tracks

The Bedouin raiders once used to cut

And slice the flanks of caravans

Along the stone-bound King's Highway,

Like wolves on the edge of an ungainly herd.

V.

Fumbling buttons on a Toshiba cassette,

An old man swept his kafiyya aside.

Confused, awkward, mystified, glanced

Up at me and hardened, crouched,

And fixed me with a polished eye:

Centuries thumbed back like prayer beads and

Again were heard bellowing camels stumbling

On the rocks, the dust was cast up thick,

Blood soaked into hungry soil, teeth glinted

Between stretched lips, the gold and the women

And the silks stripped and torn, bourn

From safety, pulled into the toothed rocks,

Into the wind and dried rain.

That polished blue eye despised

The foreigner, the gutless power

That was too soft and weak and lost.

He hated me for his abandoned ways,

Because cigarettes are not swords

And Alladin is a British stove.

And I loved him as my dream

Of what I might have been.

In the suq I always found,

Not bought, ancestral memories.

Bibles lived and walked.

Moving the Herd

The Busenitz Place, Wyoming

June, 2001

We four brushed and saddled our mounts,

I on Buster once again, a sorrel gelding

Responsive to rein more than the touch

Of knee or heel I had been accustomed to,

The taste of egg and coffee still fresh in

Our mouths, the smell of diesel exhaust

From the truck strong in the still air as

The horses stomped into the trailer to the

Clicks and slaps of their riders, the hollow

Thumps of the plank floor as the animals

Arranged themselves for the road.

We packed all four of us into the cab of the

Pick-up, I squeezed hip and thigh against a

Town boy teen tough enough to be of help,

And off we rolled, hitting fifty on the downhill

Grades of a twisting loose dirt road carrying us

The thirty miles to the Busenitz Place by seven.

We unloaded in the open ranch house yard

With two other trailers, the aluminum of the

Gates ringing like church bells loud in the still

Morning air, and folks shook hands, tightened

Cinches, and joined Wayne and his son and

Daughter leading their mounts up from the

Corral, the man all tricked out in his summer

Straw, high-heeled boots, spurs, pearl-button

Snap shirt and kerchief peeking out of his

Wranglers in the back, the real deal, and boss

Man of us all on his place.

Mounting together, eighteen riders wound up

A narrow road to a wide hogback ridge, chatting,

Loosening our bones in the saddles, the horses'

Passing gas sounding like grade-school boys in

The back of class, and after several hundred yards

We broke into an easy canter, having some distance

To cover, eighteen mounted riders moving over

The wild and broken ground with a single purpose,

Reawakening images of posses or a troop of

Cavalry hungry for capture, breaking over a rise

And pulling up, I holding my feed store cap in

The stiff Canadian wind and looking out over

A hundred miles of toothed hills, jagged ravines,

And dead and fallen ponderosa pines, their white

Twisted limbs like the bones of an innumerable

Army reaching defiantly toward the rain that

Had not come. Then Earl and I and young Jonah

Urged our mounts across the southern ridge to the

Far rim of a wide green bowl, the horizon there

Stitched by the high fence line to a crystal blue

Sky, watched three coyotes tirelessly trot along

The bowl's other rim half a mile away. Along

The stony trail above we singled out and worked

The stunted clusters of pine, boulders and twisted

Spruce, flushing the rust-brown steers and wary

Cows, many heavy-uddered and circling back

Away from their concealed calves, heading them

Down to the smoother swaths of ground veined

With tracks to the valley's floor, Buster's hooves

Scrabbling in the steep-graded screed trail, my boot

Toes loose in the stirrups, ready to clear in a roll.

We combed the cattle out of the broken scalp of

Those bony hills, trailing them down in ones and

Twos, in swelling bunches and handfuls, the horses

Cutting left and right, stepping backward on their

Haunches as recalcitrant cows had second thoughts

And tried to cut back up brush-choked ravines, or

Trotted over to pick up a missed stray hanging back

Behind a deadfall, and I looked out over the morning,

Seeing the rough brown and black trickling streams

Of cattle meandering down from steeps and troughs

Across the washes and valleys from every side, and

As we banked the flow around east and south, our
Flow merged with another and another current of
Turgid hooves, still loose and easy, aimed, leaned
By soft whoops and whistles, slaps and clicks, low
Rhythmical urgings from the riders, the herd a river
Of wooly backs and offended uums, accented by the
Bawlings of cows stepping from the flow in wait of
A lost calf trotting up.

Gently squeezing the herd of nine hundred head
Onto a steep-graded fire road not thirty feet wide
Along a wooded hillside, we coaxed and funneled
And swung those lowing heads and tails dripping with
Freshly digested grass, sang and chanted and chastised
As the dust rose from the trail into the clear morning.

Up over a rise, through two wire gates and across two
Neighbors' lands, past the late morning and into early
Afternoon we kept them moving, outriders holding the
Flow of animals within banks, cantering up as here and
There along the stream cattle sought to dribble out by the
Wayside for a shaded mouthful of dewy grass; we lost
A few dozen down a steep break into thick brush and
Low and tangled branch, I, old man Busenitz at seventy
In walking shoes and brown dress socks riding a rope-
Haltered grey, a pony-tailed barrel-racer on her bright

Bay, and a ranch boy of ten in a new cattleman straw
Riding down after them. We thrashed through the low
Growth, the sharp pistol-shots of hooves stumbling over
Or snapping deadfall branches loud in the deep shade,
Twigs and pine needles stinging our faces as we spurred
After the dodging cows, the boy, distracted, suddenly
Swept from his saddle by a low branch, deposited with
An inglorious thump upon the angled earth. Tears he had,
Breath knocked out, a scraped pink cheek, but making not
A sound shook his head in refusing our help and climbed
His mount, slapping the horse with his reins in blame.

The herd then was spread into three new pastures, driven
Deeply into the knee-high grass, and we all broke into
Mile-eating trots back to the ranch house by mid-afternoon,
Loosened cinches, put bits and bridles over horns, haltered
Our horses to their trailers, and headed laughing, dusty, and
Tired to our meal of salads and ribs, potatoes four different
Ways and half a dozen casseroles, roasts and cobblers and
Strawberry-rhubarb pies deeper than the tines of my fork.
And with thanks and handshakes and last-minute jokes and
Jabs about lost hats and fast cows and slow cowboys, we
Clicked and slapped our horses into their trailers and headed
Home, sharing the gallon jugs of drinking water warmed in
The cab all day. Back at the barn, the horses, unsaddled,
The gray-white lather hosed from their bodies, were turned

Out for a rest, and they rolled and squirmed on their backs

In the soft grass of the East Meadow. But before supper we

Loaded those rolls of wire and post drivers, the boxes of

Clips and nails into the truck—for tomorrow was fence-

Mending in the Red House Pasture.

Singularities

Gilbert

Serendipity Marina Rec Center
Palacios, Texas

Yeah, that flat plastic box behind the salt—that's it,
The saffron, that shit's like gold, pull out a few threads
Put 'em in this rice bowl, crush with a…you know what
You're doing, doancha, I add this boiling water—look at
That color, smell that steam rising—gotta have it if this
Bouillabaisse is to come out right—you on *Sarcelle,* that
C&C sloop over there, them your kids? Yeah, that's
My Catalina, just a 25 but enough for me and the old
Lady—can you mince two three those shallots real fine?
You know somethin' about fixin' food—that's good. Most
Of my shithead buddies here'll eat anything I lay down,
But they don't know nothin'. Man, I was trained, culinary
School, was a sous chef at Chez Meniere north of Houston,
We made some blue corn tortillas with braised asparagus
And duck breast seared blood rare would bring you right
Off the table.…Naw, she alright, she's a good bitch, just
With workin' in town she think she can say whatever.
Sometimes I have to, you know, straighten her out,
Smooth her down a little bit, then she okay—Oh, I got
About a quart of coquinas in the pan, got them over at
The sand bar. You can't get no clams down here, but
These tiny coquinas just make the most delicate broth.…

Yeah, they got 'em all over Florida—that where you

Been cruisin'? That's sweet—I spent some time around

Tampa, made some good money, and then this badge

Pulls me over, gave me some shit, I told him not to

Touch me, told him I wasn't no fruit picker—finally

I straightened his ass out, fixed his action, and they

Put me in for a while....Well, I did some Golden Gloves

Back in Victoria in high school but you see these thick

Eyes? I cut easy. You're right--I'm going to deglaze with

The stock but we need to strain it through this old t-shirt—

It's clean (gotta use what I can find—lotta sand and grit

In them coquinas—and now—wait—smell that saffron,

Imagine all those crocus blooms growing in Spain just

For us....Oh, I'm building fence over in Calhoun County,

Not bad cash money, no names, no taxes, no, I don't have

No car, buddy comes by—good set-up here, man: I cast

Off the lines, nobody to say nothin' about where I'm at,

Man, it's like I don't even fuckin' exist, if I don't want

To....Come back in about a hour—I'll have some French

Bread with fresh garlic and gorgonzola toasted on it to go

With the bouillabaisse—Hey, I hear that—them kids

Keep you busy....

Brother Ray

Marker One Marina

Dunedin, Florida

You want to catch a fish, boy? Dad? Can

I show him how to catch a fish, guaranteed?

Lemme see...right under here—this coffee can

Is my chum bucket, just heads and guts and fins

And skin, all chopped up, always got a bucket

On the boat, my magic soup—we'll toss a handful

Or two down into the water—yes, that was a heavy

Squall this afternoon, rain just beat the bay flat—

Yeah, that was me, washing the deck and fly bridge,

No lightning in the blow, and sure the Lord sent

All that fresh rain I might as well use it—you need

Some work done on your boat, and I do odds and

Ends around town—and I preach down in the park

And in a church over on Bayside sometimes, too,

When I can catch some ears....Well, I'll tell you:

I was down around Islamorada in the Keys, found

Me that Hatteras hull there, tore up, salvaged and

Gutted but sound, the yard let me work on it, built

The superstructure on site, and I did bottom jobs

For 'em, can work on auxiliaries in my clearer

Moments, but to say true that was not every day.

Fact is, I was in the bottle more than not, sleeping

Under the foredeck, that being the only guaranteed

Dry spot other than the engine room, and then I saw

Jean, coming out of the liquor store, I was, and

She looked, and I *saw* and she *saw*—now, me, I'm

An old dog, and she more'n fifty, pretty old and

Everything, you know, coming down, but her eyes

That blue of the Gulfstream, you've been out there

About three or four miles off Miami or the Upper

Keys, get past the buoys, Hawk Channel, the reefs

And sand spotting the bottom, and the dark turquoise

Turns to that rich deep blue, and you are in it—the

Stream, moving three to five knots across the world;

You can see the sunlight sticking down through like

An eye and the blue just goes down and down seems

Like forever—those were Jean's eyes. We talked for

Weeks, she told me how her husband died in a stupid

Car wreck, her kids all grown, and she just came

Down to get a breath of air, and I've got an ex and some

Grown kids somewhere, too, but you know I quit the

Bottle, she didn't tell me to, just looked so…well,

Disappointed, when I wanted a drink. A funny thing

Happened, too: I was feelin', you know, real hungry

One night at her motel, and so I came on, grabbin' and

Squeezin', and she put those eyes on me, said, "Don't

Make it happen; it will, if it's time," and it did, all by

Itself. Not long after that, Jean told me about the cancer,

Not sad, not mad, just smiling, like she knew something,

And then she was gone. God, I was pissed, got a bottle

Of Canadian Club...but see these hands? I looked down

And I saw one of them for the first time—they were clocks;

Me being an old Navy man, I looked at these clocks and

Sure as shit saw twenty-three hundred hours—that was

Two years ago, and that bottle's still sitting up over the

Quarter berth, looking at me. That bottle's this world

Right here, waiting for me, *wanting* me, but here's the

Thing: I came to see the day brand new fresh and clean

And *created* and I saw and see and hear and smell

The hand of God in every *thing*, in the eye of every

Man I meet, and dammit Jean was right—yeah,

"Dammit," the words don't mean anything, they're

Just words flashing by in the darkness, it's the feeling,

The knowing, that Jesus Christ is in every god damned

Blessed barnacle under my keel, they are just words

Of feeling—He knows—even when I'm alone and

Meet a woman and me not entirely dead belowdecks,

But He was human, and to be human he would have

Known. To have died and doubted, hanging there,

"Why have you forsaken me?"—He had to learn the

Doubt, too, if he was to understand what it was like

To be human, and so when I fall I can still see that

Gulfstream in my eyes—hey, I gotta go pick up a

Part before they close—he'll get one. Just put the

Chum bucket in the cockpit—bless you, Cap!

Iliana,

In Southern Bulgaria

I leaned against the wall, cuestick in hand,
And watched a game, when with a man she walked in,
In loose jeans and white blouse, and she sat and
Turned and seized my eye, and caught my breath
As if I were a naughty child, and I saw the short
Hair framing the face, cheekbones clear and sharp,
Lips sculpted underneath a porcelain nose, and
Deep brown eyes as old as the earth, as simple
And strong as tooth whittling bone, a wisdom of
Body and instinct, eyes speaking in a thousand years
Of history, older, telling of the power to send
A nation to war, eyes to make one kill or die for....

And I was propelled, hell, driven, drawn, as by
An irresistible hand, to look again, and again,
To search for those eyes, to seek them regardless
Of risk, and I was terrified--of what those eyes
Might make me do, to others, to myself.

Route 35

Texas Gulf Coast

You touch that door handle one more time and I'll
Chop your fingers off and eat them like sausages.
Think it's connected, anyway? If I were stupid, you
Wouldn't be sitting here, would you? "Extras for a
Pepsi commercial," for God's sake—who's the idiot?
Killing someone isn't difficult, nor is escaping.
Just out-reason the reasoner. Ah, vacation...me,
I've done this coast for six years now

No, I may not. That pretty blonde hair—you could
Always get away, humm, maybe even talk me out
Of it. Like what, what do you have to support what
I want to do? Money I don't need. What I don't
Understand is why those terrorist assholes, with
A real taste for it, why follow somebody else's
Directions. Choose? Why you? Because, baby,
I don't know who the hell you are. Hey, discrimination
Is against the law—me, I'm indiscriminant. You
Breathe, you're game. What reason? Sweetheart,
You haven't been listening. "What's the motive,
What's the connection, what's the pattern, the reason"—
Those are questions a thinking investigator asks,
but with one fatal flaw, assuming, assured, that the

Perpetrator,—uh, actor, they say now not to be

Prejudicial, uses reason and logic, has a pattern,

That human animals are driven by those directives

Most of us are haunted by—and that's where the law

Is stupid and self-centered, and blind.

Not that I expect you to serve as my amanuensis to

Posterity--my recorder, you idiot! I'm just fucking

Talking to myself here, sixty miles an hour, middle

Of the fucking night, Rockport in the mirror—

See this guy fishing? Let's see if he knows....Shut

The fuck up—you do anything, I'll pop you both

Right here—"Hey, buddy, how far to...."

See, babe? Buh-bye—pop pop—they're baby nipples,

Pacifier nipples--a little irony there, hey, Charlene?

I don't care if it's not your name—it is now. A new

World, isn't it? See how it is, stop, call him over,

Just a couple of pops with a nipple over the end of

The barrel, and we're on our way—"Lord, I was

Born a travellin' ma'an...."

Let's do some sex, babe. Hell-oh-ho?

You want to do it alive or dead? Believe me,

Darlin', I can make it happen either way, and

If your heart isn't in it, I'll just pop-pop and make
Up the sounds myself.

Ooooo, yeah. I know about this road here....
See where we can just pull over down past these
Blackjack oaks where the old roofing is piled?
I still can't believe the way people just dump crap
Wherever....Now one wrist to this little pine
Here--don't fight me, Charlene. Doesn't that resin
Just smell like a fresh oil painting?

A Stripper's Surgery

After Miss Tiffany pumped soft and kitteny offstage
In her plexiglass platforms, a scarlet robe swirling
Around her thighs, she sat at the mirror, pile of
Rumpled bills in a basket, and knew it was time
For honing, for reloading, for Dr. Jack....

First the breasts, she wanting more cleavage,
So out came the flat yellow bags of old silicone
Or saline or whatever in literal hell it was, laid
Out like veal chops for display, and into the flaccid
Empty sags of breast, beneath the nipple in a time-
Worn cut were stuffed the clean and new and
Larger tighter bags of belief, as if her body were
A flak jacket or bulletproof vest to be packed with
Pad and armor, deflecting injury, a wall between
Wearer and world.

Next the betadine-smeared thighs, where the
Liposuction wand probed down and back, down
And back inside those velvety thighs, the probe
Stretching out the skin as an index finger might
In a cheek to make a funny popping sound, no
Grins here as clear vinyl tubing filled and
Coughed and filled again with pink and white
Subcutaneous fat that might mar some trucker's
Dream of exciting daughter or neighbor's or

Stranger's child into a writhing squirm of
Abandoned bestiality.

And after all was done and drained away,
After Tiffany was tucked and sucked and
Plumped again, as the bliss of administered
Coma wore into wakefulness, Miss Tiffany
Started, jumped and bucked on the table as
If seized in the claws of a demon's hand, no
Lazarus she, knowing she had been beyond
Control in a stranger's grip, having so much
Self stolen before.

More Papers

Cooper Villa Senior Living Community
Mrs. Janet Gennoway to her mother

> "O reason not the need! Our basest beggars
> Are in the poorest things superfluous.
> Allow not nature more than nature needs,
> Man's life is cheap as beasts...."
> —*King Lear,* II, iv

"O, just sign it, Mom. I SAID SIGN HERE! DO YOU
HAVE YOUR HEARING AID IN? I may as well be talking
To myself anyway. Half the time you call me Blanche, the
Sister who died twenty years ago. I SAID WE'RE TAKING
CARE OF IT FOR YOU—THE RAILROAD RETIREMENT,
MOM. Good thing Dad had that job, God knows we couldn't
Have you living with us—I've changed enough diapers in
My day—at least the children are pleased with themselves,
Burbling away and laughing as the mess comes out—you're
So ashamed and embarrassed I want to cry, I SAID WE'LL
TRY AND COME ON SATURDAY but Bill has his golf
Game and I have to get my roots done at La Laine's, I SAID
WAYNE'S RETIRING, and Bobby and Samantha are both
Driving up from San Marcos on Spring Break, separate cars,
Of course, and both of them will want to go to Papadeaux,
And, Mama, you know you'd rather stay here, you get so

Upset in places like that with all those people pushing

Around, I SAID I FOUND A TOAD IN THE POOL—

MOM, YOU *KNOW* WE HAVE A POOL—and Bill needs

To replace the pump and get new tires, so I need to transfer

Some from that mutual fund you turned over to us last year,

But you don't need that—nothing to worry about—we've

Got you now. God, don't you even see the mashed potatoes

On your blouse? They really need to take better *care* of her.

I SAID WHERE IS THAT ROBE WE GAVE YOU? HERE,

MOM, HOLD THE PEN—DON'T CRY, MOMMA—I'LL

FIND IT. What are you waiting on? You don't want to eat,

You don't watch TV, you won't go to the exercise or games

Classes—you can't even get up and get dressed without help....

You remind me of Schatzie sometimes, I hate to put it like

That, but you remember Schatzie, our miniature Schnauzer,

Oh, she was our love for so long, so spoiled she was a foot

Tall at the shoulder but lying on her back had a twenty-inch

Waist, and then the hearing went, and then the cataracts,

Bumping into the table legs, you could hear her, and then

One morning the hips gave out and she couldn't get up—

You made *me* take her to Dr. Hart for the end, couldn't

Drive, you said, CAN'T DRIVE NOW, I SAID, MOM,

YOU KNOW WE'LL TAKE YOU WHERE YOU NEED

TO GO. Only one more paper, and those railroad checks

Are deposited directly into our account, so much better

Access, we can close that last account. I SAID THE

47

AMOUNT WE ARE PAYING HERE IS TOO MUCH.
YOU CAN WEAR THAT BLOUSE TOMORROW, TOO,
And you won't even know we're gone in May, it's just
Ten Days, Rose Hill says they can keep her in the
Cooler for two weeks, until we get back, if you go while
We're on the cruise—I SAID YOU SHOULDN'T USE
ALL THAT PAIN MEDICINE, and with these headaches
I've been getting—I'LL BE BACK SOON, MAMA. I
LOVE YOU. I do.

An Unfortunate Encounter with a Lady

Lake Grapevine

So often, a lazy fisherman, I let the nickel-sized
Breadball down, near the bottom, brace the rod
On the dock and wander off, to sand or caulk, stitch
Or snug down, sometimes sleep on my tethered boat.

And one June morning, stepping off *Sarcelle* into the
Dappled dawn, waiting while a heron strode with sticky
Feet off the pier, I noted the tight strand of line, the
Rod's gentle arc, telling of another world connected
Inexorably to my liminal hour. The line led down to
The milky jade of twenty feet below, to cat or carp or
Confused bass or bream big as a dinner plate....

I plucked up my ferruled bow, set my feet, and reared
Back, feeling a dogged pull and then dead weight and
Saw in the mind's eye an old mudcat thrice wrapped
About a sunken limb, and I pulled and reeled, pulled
And reeled up the discouraging burden toward the day
Until I saw, the webbed toes paddling, a soft-shelled
Turtle big as a serving dish, her delicate neck and pointed
Snout looking for all my world a dowager in offended
Distress—and I a thoughtless thug, cheap blade in
Hand, dragged her by the head, leery of the snap of jaws
I knew some could send, her fanning feet finding no

Purchase in air or, after I stood on her shell, on the rough
Concrete of the dock.

She struggled on, wagging her weary head, the soft
Wrinkled neck distended and vulnerable behind an
Elongated brow, the tiny nostrils foremost, and then
The eyes slow-blinking in pain, my mustad gold-toned
Hook fixed firmly in her mouth, the blood, if ever
Innocent blood were shed, leaking in undiluted strands
To the makeshift stone below.

And hemostat in hand, I fixed barbed hook and began
To twist, the cartilage resisting my misbegotten attempts
At relief, blood smearing a jaw and face wrenched awry
In brute force, her eye all the while impassive to a world
Where suffering is commonplace.

With a final turn and crisp snap of broken flesh, I
Freed my battered captive and sent her down, hoping
The wound would not fester into slow death, the pain
I felt out of all proportion to the sportsman I should
Be. She had taken no pleasure in my world, and I none
In hers. And I fished no more that day, nor the next.

Soldiers

A Voice from the Chapel:

Mission San Antonio de Valero; March 6, 1836

Colonel James Bowie to his Slave

Where we die there's always rock and sky;

These walls, this earth and dirt—the old fox

Has run to ground, tooth and all.

Sam, hand old Mas'Jim that jug there--

You recall where this blade here

First found home in some man's ribs?

God, times I thought this steel pushing

Me west, quivering like a divining rod

But I see the tiny shells frozen here

In these dry stone blocks, and the pens,

The slave pens out on Galvez haunt me still;

The eyes of black faces rolling like worlds,

The waves washing nothing clean, not

Jean Lafitte smirking like an old babbon,

Fingering a stolen saber, selling souls

By the pound—and me buying a round

Bundle, too, under that sweaty sky.

Go, Sam--I set you free. Leave me

To dance that damned dequello

Blown for us all, for the mission, the cause,

The call of men hungry for the ground,

Hungry to be sold into oblivion . . . .

No, leave the cob—me and the whiskey

Will race like old horses gone lame;

Why did I hostage my name to those

Arkansas acres, to Ursula's promise of peace,

To the fame of a cloud-gray blade

Made from a piece of falling sky?

Dammit, Sam—why do I lie here

On these greasy Kiowa rags, on this bag

Of corn husks for a cot, waiting to be shot

Or stuck by some indio zapadore?

I could have opened one belly more

And not be rustling here, coughing

And groaning like a lung-shot buck,

Here to end, with two trembling children

And a sack of breathing property

That may be but has not been;

God, Sam—the chains, the men,

The days spent like coins....

The Wilderness,

Near Spotsylvania Court House
Spring, 1864

The ripening red of the huckleberry
Was six inches from my opened eye, and
My senses swam back like lazy carp
In a muddy pond, and I smelled the mold
Beneath the needles of second growth pine
That cushioned my cheek, heard the hum
Of flies, and a crackling of bacon frying,
Until my mind cleared the sound into
Distant musket fire....

I watched as my grey-sleeved arm
Wandered over from some remote rest
And I stretched jaws in an open-mouthed
"Ahh" as foreign-feeling fingers touched
A crust of broken scalp and the grate
Of splintered bone—my God, the crown
Of my head, like a torn cantaloupe rind,
And whispers swirled round inside: "Cap'n,
Them's Hancock's boys, a damn regimen'..."
"I am counting on your men, Captain..."
"Sargeant, stand, and fire at will..."
As the smoke from distant brush fires
Burned my eyes and we could see only half

A stone's throw between hickory saplings
And twisted old oak, and the other whispers
Now: "John, please come back—I can't handle
These boys alone, but I get so tired sometimes
Being the good and the hard one, too, punishing
And comforting," and I rolled onto my back,
As a bluejay screamed derisively at me
Like an old woman whose floor I had just
Muddied, the jay telling me by her presence
The fighting, and my men, had moved away
And I was alone.

But I rolled to the side, groaned into sitting,
But saw the arm of Daniel Humphrey, that ugly
Pewter ring on his finger; "Dan, we're left,"
I said, and reached for a shoulder that was
Not there, a body gone, and felt the pounding
Pulse at my head, and wondered where the
Rest of Daniel was, how careless he had been
To leave this just lying about....

Al-Husn,

in Northern Jordan

The tell rises like a mesa, wind-smoothed,

Above a village of concrete and brown stone—

Two state-run petrol pumps, red topped;

A row of hollow shops on the Jarash road,

A white, chipped police shed, two guards seated

Outside in back-tilted chairs, their gray-blue

British wools broken by silver stripes and badges,

Laughing, smoking, and sipping tea from glasses,

Watching the lorries labor by on their way

To Mafraq or Damascus, grinding gears, belching

Rich, oily spoor into the wind, past the bare

Hard hillside stacked with one-story poured

Cubes of concrete four meters square,

Mud-daubers' nests on a shelf in Judea,

The interstices here and there flapping

With the flags of pants and skirts, shirts

And scarves in livid pink and chartreuse,

As if to mock the hot, dry hills with color.

Al-Husn Camp: for forty years a cistern dry

Of hope, a stamp for landless feet, a station

For those who cannot go up or back,

For those orphans too knowing to rear,

Who are always no older than ten, who

Cross a border on the buttocks of a friend

Or clutch the bombs of a brother's dream;

There is no other way, it seems, to be

Other than someone everyone wants dead.

The boxes rest peaceably, scattered on the hill

Like magazines spilled from a munitions crate,

Waiting for the practiced hands, shouted

Orders, urgently whispered commands . . . .

Lina Elias Owais, Shahir Homoud, Qasim Koufali,

Hiyam Al-Nashash, Suhir Tarrar, Muhummed Abu-Gassim,

Skin thin as parchment, thin as promises,

Thin as waiting lists for passports, for change,

Skin stretched tight as the belly of an

Expectant cat, the lives squirming underneath,

Hungry for the light and air, for prey

Bassam Iseed, Abdollah Bayeg, Ahlam Al-Madoun,

Waiting, thin-skinned, behind the tell

Whose worth in potsherds and broken tools

Archeologists from five countries

Are so eager to unearth.

St. Archangel Cemetery

Plovdiv, Bulgaria, 1992

Lance Corporal E. Roskell, Royal Lancaster Regiment,
Died 17 July, 1917; Private H. Livermore, Hampshire,
6 March, 1916, age 20; Captain A.B.G. Biggerton-Evans,
South Wales Borderers, age 26—all fifty five swept up
After the Great War, "having perished in captivity,"
Debris of the Salonika Campaign....

Maybe sixty by eighty feet the plot is, a placket of soil
With tended grass, grass as green as forgotten sheep-folds,
And bordered and spaded, planted with red roses and framed
With a waist-high wall mortared cleaner and tighter than
The city hall; and the graves, row upon low and quiet row,
Angled their polished, granite faces into the cloudy day.
And somehow among these now and forever expatriots, I am
At home, the old chums all around me laugh and clack
Mug against mug...until I see along the bar the bones
Jutting through the rotted uniforms, and teeth nevermore
To meet in meal or kiss, in this private pub, forever and
Only their own; I listen and hear the muffled voices:

"Remember, Georgie? Remember when here they dragged our
Bones in '19 an' read those words of that old sod Brooke,
Him that never even got here but sickened and died

59

On the way? What'd he know of lying here, though I thought
I heard some fellow say how he's coming apart on some island
Not too far—'there's some corner of a foreign field,' says
Old Rupert, 'That is forever England.' Bloody hell, mates,
Wha' do you say to that, eh? And he says there's some eternal
Mind sending thoughts and dreams and laughter from England
Our way. Hear 'em, lads? What do you say to that, Mister
Private Michael Finnerty, you that was lying behind that
Farmhouse up near the monastery in the Rhodopes since—
When–April of '16? I recall you telling us how after
Being in the damp three years in that poplar box, the
Damn thing come apart in the handling and off went a pig
With your arm—and did they run after those wriggling hams,

Eh? What thoughts of England were those?....Hush, boys.
Listen—someone's clumb over the steps into our little
Pub o' stones here—hear him, lads? A Yank, two of 'em,
Two bloody Yanks. At least we can make out what they're
Sayin'. Thought for sure was more gypsy kids come to
Snuffle those bags o' glue—them little sods get loony,
Eh, Mike?" But a magpie screamed from a broken stone,
And I heard no more, the eyes welling full, I hoped
Half for them, I knew at least half for me,
A bit close to the ground myself.

A Confederate on the Square

Columbia, Tennessee

Our own stone private there, I saw such a man,
And nine more, when the First Tennessee
Moved to Virginia the first year of the War.

Up past Hampshire Crossing we had marched,
The day a wet and ugly grey, even past noon
The sleet rattling against our leather cartridge
Pouches like thrown rice or wheat chaff,
The twin jets of steam pumping rhythmically
From the caisson mules' dripping nostrils,
As we wound and twisted our way up the
Steep valley seamed with St. John's Run,
Up through sparse stands of hickory and gum,
Iron-black fingers of bare branches reaching
Arthritically, in supplication, toward
An unfeeling sky....

We marched two-by-two when there was room,
Smartly, for the warmth, breathing into our
Mufflers, our eyes watering with the scratch
Of wool and file of frost, our ankles wrapped
In rags, we marched in deep silence, with one
Crow telling all the world of our passing, a metal

Click of shod hoof on infrequent stone swallowed
Up in the sleet-sheathed afternoon.

The Third Arkansas Regiment we had come
To relieve, they, watching this way for almost
Three days, would be ready to move down to
The banked fires and frying biscuits of the
Main army. And we topped a ridge fringed
In young jack pine, the needles coated thick
Almost as fingers with the ice, waited for the
Challenge and grateful grin of soldiers finding

Friends not foes, when beyond the ridge opened
Before us the grey and brown clad men so still
And unmoving, not turning their grizzled heads
Or arms raised in cheer or voiced challenge to
Our brusque intrusion, as one man stood near
A lightning-split chestnut, musket at parade rest,
His swaddled shoulders turned away from me
In the chill....

        still in my dreams I see his face
As I rounded on him, arm on his sleeve, and
Felt and heard the crunch, as of crushed leaves
Underfoot, the crackling of frozen tunic, and
Looked up into his marble face, an icicle frozen
Down from the tip of his strong-boned nose

62

Across the grey and long-silenced lips, on past

A smoothed-down growth of reddish beard, to

A shiny and graceful point from his chin, in

My dreams I see his polished cheeks, lashes

Sparkling with the frost, and hear the frozen rain

Patter on the frozen man, a sentinel still.

He and nine other men found we there,

Having become stone in their cause;

And here and there amongst the living,

In South and North, still

Do we watch for the dead.

A Cardinal's War

Beaumont Holiday Inn

An oasis off the atrium, outside the hotel café,
We could see it through the relective glass,
A respite of camellia and palm, fern and photinia,
A crimson fluttering and stop, a wheeling flicker
Of bright feathers, as a cardinal flew from a nearby
Branch and smashed blindly into the mirrored
Windows, clutched the sill, flew up and slammed
Again, over and over, down and back, slap and
Peck, resting on a branch for some moments before
Beginning the attack again.

The bird was fighting an impervious foe there
In the glass, his own reflection taken to be rival,
Competition for his blessed spot meant no doubt
To be dukedom for his bride, as my colleague,
Passing, noted with a superior mile, "We can see
Where the expression 'bird brain' originates," and
Moved on, but I remained hypnotized by the fight's
Futility, the contest that could not be won, and I
Wondered for how long, how many times, I waged
War in my smug competition, my implacable foe,
When I fought no more than that selfsame reflection
Of myself.

Returning the Colors

Reunion of the Fifth Georgia Regiment

Macon, Georgia

Friday, August 1, 1884

So inexplicable now looking out at your creased and
Kindly faces, I, Captain L.C. Young, recall that twenty
Years ago I would have shot dead any one or all of you,
And you would have done the same for me. But today,
As you have heard, I would do you some service.
Let us remember:

South Carolina, it was, November 6th, 1864, what has
Come to be called the Battle of Fort Coosahatchee, with
Savannah scarcely thirty miles to our south. I recall the
Cool early morning hours of that day—being from New
York, and at that time a private in the Fifty-sixth New York
Regiment under General Foster, I cannot say it was *cold*
For a November morning but that damp sticky cool here
In the South, with a bit of swamp mist drifting through
The open spaces between the brush, and threads—even
Wraiths of it wandering over the dark surface of that
Coosahatchee River, and out of the cloak of near-dawn
Air came a voice: "Hey, Blue boy, you boys got some
Coffee over there?" the Southern drawl as languid as the
River's surface sliding by. "Yeah, Johnny, you need some,

Send over some of that sweet cane sugar you got piled
Back there." And so we made bundles of brown homespun
And arched them over to the opposite banks, and a soldier
From each side snuck out for the trade, half-expecting the
Punch of a Minnie ball through his tunic before returning
To the safe morning fire—you recall that?

How had we come to this—and how far returned from
That brink I cannot say nor am seeking an answer here.
I see in many of your faces, and in your limbs and bodies,
You wear the War Between the States each aching day,
And I see in your eyes the swollen numbers who cannot
Be with us today. Our morning fires are steep banked and
Grow dim, but let me remind you not of the pain nor the
Disappointment of what has passed but of that sometime
Shining day when we met fair foes.

Early afternoon, my repeater said, but the chill of the
Morning was held close down by a tight blanket of
Unmoving cloud. The Fifty-sixth New York had ferried
Across, you recall, on shag log rafts back behind that
Tight meander of the river east of your position, and we
Filled in the hardwoods along the cut bank, setting up
Positions and digging. Your captain, William Horsley,
I since have learned, sent you across that open ground
Time and time again to push us from the trees, and

66

Back across the river, and as though it was yesterday
I see you boys rushing across that ground, dodging the
Palmetto fronds lashing at your pumping legs, your
Rebel yells ringing out like the dogs of hell were coming
At us, and the sounds and smell of your firing and ours,
The smell of burning powder and scorched cloth patches,
I still can smell that fine candle scent from the beeswax
Our lieutenant sealed his revolver loads with, and the dead
And the not yet dead....And in the grays and browns and
Plumes of dirty white smoke, the drab sweep of day, your
Battle flag, your colors, your cause such a bright patch of
Blood red in that filthy shambles, we had to have it.
Like boys shouldering close to a ring drawn on the dirt,
To play for that marble that outshone all the rest, we leaned
Forward and shot for your color guard.

Five times, you will bear me witness, I see them falling in
My dreams, if you can call those hauntings by such a name,
One of your men thrust forward, the flag held in advance,
As if ideas could be spears, two hands gripping, and the right
Hand always uppermost, the fabric waving with the speed
Of the charge, that being the only wind that day, and first
Thomas Brantley, I later needed to give each dancer a
Clearer face, was brought down by a bullet to his breast,
But before he fell the staff tottered, was caught and carried
On by Thomas Barney, until, can any other than we ever

Comprehend the macabre look of innocent surprise caught
On a man's face when struck full in the throat by a musket
Ball? As Private Barney angled down to the sodden earth,
Lieutenant William Harp, scarcely a man in age, stepped,
Knelt, and thrust again high that badge of bursting heart.
We had never seen the like, nor would think to see again.

And yet again, over the corduroyed afternoon, William Hart
Emerged at the fore of your skirmish line, the stars and bars
Working with the steam of his churning legs, the Fifth
Georgia pushing apace, perhaps scenting a weakened line,
Baying like excited hounds after a sighted coon, but we
Were fishing for you wily dogs this time, flanking your
Field with Company E, pouring ball and shot and sharp-
Shooters on from the east and north, some of us freshly
Armed with those Spencer carbines, opening and closing
Our hands in those curved levers and firing almost as fast
As clapping our hands, we yelling back and cursing, all
Of you grudgingly turning, dragging your bleeding sons,
Wisely ordering a guarded retreat, the bugles like threads
Of sound winding amongst the whistle and whine of ball
And bullet, the plea of a fallen friend, your line pulling
Back, leaving dead for the truced reclaiming, past the gashed
And broken ground, until, like a frighted deer washed up
On a sandbank after a river's flood withdrawn, Harp
Looked about and found himself and your flag alone.

We did not know whose ball shattered his ankle and carried
Half his boot away, the splinters of bone visible to us all,
But Caleb McCrimmon caught him first, finishing with
His bayonet the rolling of that proud eye. And it was Caleb
Who gathered in the colors of the day. Bivouacked two weeks
Later we were, and Corporal McCrimmon holding what he
Knew an iron hand, kings over sevens, stronger than his
Sheaf of Yankee dollars he had peeled from over the course
Of a late night game, when down I snapped one eight, and
Then another, and then a third, and collected that crimson
Prize.

That was twenty years ago, as each one of you well knows,
Twenty long years but only a brief moment in memory as
I see your eyes light up with what my hands hold. I have
Dreamt of this day since that dripping winter tent held our
Grave exchange. Captain Turner, please accept now this
Emblem of your cause and but scant and storied reminder
Of the courage all of you unfolded to us that day. We the
Fifty-sixth New York by agreement and with admiration
Return your colors and are at rest.

Simplicities

A Box of Crabs

Two dozen blue-claws in a Delmonte box
That once carried cans of cream-style corn,
Two dozen clattering hands scraping and
Thumping in a dry darkness unlike the depths -
And we bundled them up the fire stairs in
The hot Florida afternoon, set the stock pot
On to steam, Robin sliding the blues
Into the corner to quiet down....

And when the boil was rolling seeds and spices
Fast, together we tipped the clicking claws and
Fan-blade legs into the steam, slammed down
The lid, and went to watch the game where
Mowatt caught the pass, shed tacklers like
Clods of dried mud, and...with a sharp bang
And the cacophonous ring of aluminum on tile,
We yelled and ran for the stove, only to see
Bodies roil out of the pot, tumble to the floor,
And scuttle sideways, claws extended, like
Knife fighters in a fifties street rumble.
Some half dozen still rolled, orange and brown
In the steam, left behind like trampled fans
At a soccer match, the rowdies uncaring,
Taken to the streets for destruction.

Robin and I rounded them up, many draped in

Cobwebs and flies' bodies from beneath

The cabinets, one wearing an old roach trap

Like some thick African amulet, another

Dragging a forgotten crouton shrouded in lint.

Well, we pamplonaed them with spatulas and spoons

And sent them back into the pot, debris and all.

Minutes later, on newsprint, they were snapping

Open under the nutcracker's jaws, the flesh

Shiny and almond white, plunged without mercy

Into blue carp rice bowls of melted butter,

Bobby Bowden's Seminoles beating the drums

Toward a TD.

As a Boy,

Near Lake Lanier

Sharp, red sand gritted in my wet sneakers
As I wound through hickory and oak, reaching
A granite-graveled road lined on each side
With the leafy and bristled arches of blackberries
Hanging thick and swollen as grapes, breaking open
Under my busy fingers, the wet and sticky wine
Of the summer rain oiling the soiled creases of
Hours'-old hands as I gobbled along toward a
Warping dock knee-deep in the jade-milked
Water of the lake.

Squatting under the hot tin of the boathouse,
I opened the brown cardboard of the worm box
And dug my fingers in through the peat, through
The dark mystery of the earth, and found a tight
Constricting form pulling back from my touch,
My monkey fingers wriggling through to the living
Thing, seizing, feeling it break and spill yellow
And green, spill the scent of life and food so
Strong I was drawn to snap it up on the spot, but
Twisted human-like away and punctured the tube
Of squeezing nerves over and over onto the hook;
The bobber waited on the shaded water's surface
As I smelled my fingers like a dog.

75

Smelling salt in an on-shore breeze

I remember eating spiny reef lobster

down on Plantation Key when I was a kid,

the creatures snapping and creaking as we

tossed them into a four-gallon pot, boiling

with seawater, and slammed down the lid,

holding it so they wouldn't spring to safety

before turning spotted rust to sunset scarlet

in the steam. Then we'd slap each down

on a cutting board, lay a butcher knife lengthwise

between the haired legs, and hit that knife

with a hammer, exposing that flesh

to the world.

The yellow melamine plate held a laid-open lobster,

a cup of melted butter, and a quartered candy-

smelling key lime ready. Somehow I always

gashed a finger on a shell spine so that when

I squeezed the juice, part of a lobster bite was

the sharp sting of citrus in a cut, the rest the

flesh of lobster tail clean, smooth, springy under

dry teeth, the taste iodine and shrimp,

fire coral and cherrystone clam. I would

work my tongue over the shreds of flesh,

hear the cry of a great blue heron outside,

and want for nothing more.

I still don't.

Cicadas

There's something George C. Scott
About a cicada, looking like a helmetted
Tank commander rolling inexorably forward,
Up and out of seventeen years underground,
Years of burrowing in darkness, of nursing
Sweet sap from swollen breasted roots, of
Isometric flexing and pumping hydraulic
Fluids beneath a brown-husked placenta
Carapace...

A diesel among insects, he buzz-rumbles
Up into my hardshell pecan, singing the
Dry hundred-degree evening for a moment's
Bliss, a moment's kiss of death, before tumbling
To the concrete, a file of ants marking the spot
Next morning as his lover prepares her eggs
For the allure of the cooling darkness.

Oh, armored harbinger, what new world
Will your children know, what new sun
Rise in that time?

Dung Beetles

Goose Island, Texas

Shiny black and nimble-legged,
The beetle pushed ball and driving beetle, too,
The driver clinging spread-eagled as the sand-
Brown ball rolled this way and that amongst
The pathside debris—past glossy rust-brown
Ovals of live oak leaves, over large-grained grey
Sand and broken fossilized oyster shell until
Brought up short and solid in the fork of
A fallen twig, the house-high ball of dung
Built and smoothed, rounded with the delicate
Touch of a potter's care over a month of beetle-
Days stuck unmoving.

The driver beetle fidgeted at the helm,
The pusher pushed port and starboard, fore
And aft, leaning right and left like a tired boxer
Weaving in thought about the next assault, and
Then down drove the beetle beneath broken bits
Of leaves and bark, tunneling them upward as
Underneath the ball and his driving mate he thrust,
Pulsing and shouldering upward in exo-skeletal
Force the immense weight of dirt and dung until
It rolled out and over the imprisoning twig, and

Without even a moment to gather breath or

Congratulation, he rolled friend and globe

Hastily on.

The Ant Lions

At recess, sometimes I stood near the door,
The outside door, of my fourth grade class,
Amongst the black loam brought in and mixed
With the coral sand into a charcoal grey, the
Violet periwinkles scrunched into a rich purple
And then black near the center, the deep green
Waxy leaves looking tough and clean; and down
Where the tendrils of St. Augustine reach
Crab-like to the limits of their thirst for
Water and for light, where the dusty sand
Is mounded and dimpled by the steps of shoes,
A gnawed number-two pencil cast down,
I saw the world I was a god upon:

Ant lions, doodle bugs some say,
Though too silly a name for ferocity,
So clever and patient and concealed,
So predatory and terrible, poised,
Waiting there in the motionless sand,
Jaws dry and gaping, waiting for some
Blind beast to stumble and scrabble
on the edge of the inexorable whorl....

So simple and quiet in the grey sand,

They wait, flicking out grains of incident

And waste, hulls of the fall....

Mud Daubers

s/v *Capricorn*

Fort Myers Municipal Marina

Beneath the fiddled shelf in the cabin,
Inside the sail cover left too long,
Behind the wet locker's louvered door
Their adobe urns await....

One waved out the companionway
Drops a wet globe on the bridgedeck,
One dead and dried in the galley sink
Tells of a breezeless day unbearable.

The marina's anasazi,
Cliff dwellers in our crafts' chiaroscuro,
Building birth urns from sticky spheres
Of earth flown how many wasp miles
From river bank to slip....

I could love them more had I
No need to clean their cradles.

A Sailboat's Spiders

Dawn

Decks and cabin top, lifelines and draping sheets
Dripping in the first light, the jewelling dew
Diamonding bracelets between breeze-swept angles,
The drops glittering in the last moment of luxury
But scattered and sprinkled, as if by some lapidary's
Cool design, in the webs are caught the emerald
Shine and quiet lapis gleam of fly or burnished
Beetle, delicate gnat or enameled wasp, in a brief
Time of sparkling elegance, quickly dying,
Before burning away in the rising sun....

Underway

The sloop heels in the bright day,
And from its shrouds and stays, streaming out
Singly up and down the wires, in the breeze,
The strands of spider web are trolled in an
Ocean of air, glistening filaments swinging wide
On the bright breaths of the morning, their
Fishers waiting for the touch, the tremble of
Leg or wing, to gather in the catch and spin it
Into a silky sleep.

At Rest

As the hull swings and wheels at anchor,
Slowly winding between breeze and tide,
The sun seemingly pulled down of its own
Weight toward a beard of palm and sea, after
A simple meal of rice, tinned meat and fruit,

Tumbler of garnet wine in hand, I glance
At gossamered corners, draped belowdeck
Joinings where my velvet fellows weave
Tight garments for the insects of the night,
Mosquitoes and sandflies and hummng gnats
That would steal the comfort of my sleep,
And I am grateful.

The Mallards

Scott's Landing Marina

Most are quiet couples,
The wives in wild-rice tweed, brooches of
Lapis lazuli blue on each wing, the husbands
Politely gliding behind in suede grey and
Brown cape, white clerical collar and elegant
Emerald heads—oh, they are proud pairs
Wagging and waddling down the piers past
The impassive prows of towering sailboats,
Sometimes seeming to hike imaginary skirts
Or trouser legs before dropping off the
Concrete walk into the waiting lake;
And there, there amongst the white crumbles
Of styrofoam and algae-bearded twigs, through
Faded floating cans and a broken bobber,
The pair glides out as on silver skates, low
Wakes veeing behind their quiet passage...

But down near the gate, where several breeds
Wait the passing of children with popcorn and
Old bread, a trio of trim mallard teens, tough,
Their breasts thrust out, push through the
Breeze-ruffled lake, the lead bravado with
Bright orange legs and shining cap loudly

Announcing their presence, his fellow to port

Sporting a younger green head still pimpled

In brown down. A faint scent of English Leather

And Marlboros follows their wake.

Duco Cement

The redolent vapor wells up the past—
It should have killed the Sphinx moth,
Wondrous addition to my collection, but
It didn't, the velvet cocoa fur of the moth's
Body and dust of her wing, the eye
Inscrutable as a found Sioux bead on an
Ant mound in the field, pinioned to the
Killing board with a steeled straightpin
Through the thorax.

She should have died that first day
But she did not—wiggling her wiry legs
She gripped the foam board—I could
Hear the claws scrabbling—and I gave her
The thick drop of cement from the metal
Tube, coating the head, ignorant at ten
The spiracles breathed life beneath the
Soft flexing abdomen, and the vapor stung
My pink nostrils, I knew the power of the
Poison and was sure.

But it did not die. And on the third day,
Born of frustration, I salved the body in
The viscous glue and was at last satisfied

The tiny, tiny life was stilled, feeling no

Victory, no glory of capitulation, but

Shame at the loss of so great a life.

At Anchor,

Tres Palacios Bay

With mosquitoes lurking in the lees,

We are so blessed with the breeze

The First Snow

Plovdiv, Bulgaria, 1992

After a light rain it began,
Tentatively at first, a tiny patter
Of feet down the sky, not staying,
Making no mark on the greys and browns
Of walkway, road, and rough soil, testing,
The snow unsure whether time had come,
Then deciding, unburdenindg, in its rush,
Lemming-like, to shroud the dark earth
In the ceremony of apparent innocence.

Signs

Rooster Bridge

Demopolis, Alabama, 1919

See that leghorn out by the chinaberry there?
That's what started the whole thing, a damn-fool
Chicken out at Jack Deegan's place, strutting
And jutting out its head and pecking probably
Some corn that wasn't even there, just out
Of habit, getting between Bob McCaslin's feet
As he stepped off the porch and headed for
The spring-house for maybe another jug.
He tripped, it squawked, feathers flew,
And I leaned back in my chair and laughed
And said that if we could pay for that bridge
With chickens, we could buy it tomorrow.
Well, we nodded and laughed and pulled on pipes,
Until old Jack says maybe I got something there,
And we knew we were in trouble since old
Jack could sell you your own teeth, and add
An installation charge. And when he said
We could buy a bridge across the Tombigbee
River, with maybe not hens but cocks,
We smelled a swindle coming.

Old Jack said we'll hold an auction and sell
Every rooster we can get, and get some special

Famous roosters, but the only

Celebrity cock I could recall was a grown

Dyed Easter chick gone in the head, if most

Aren't gone already, that pecked old

Sheriff Henry's girl once too often on the legs,

And Henry shot that crazy green bird,

The bullet moving on, glancing off some flint,

And finding the right eye of his prize bull,

A day that black beast has never forgot.

Well, we forgot Deegan's plot until

Frank Derby, down at the Post Office, says

We need to donate maybe a dozen shoats

Because we ought to have a barbeque

To go along with the auction out at Moscow Ferry

And me and Bob and Willie and Earl Pace,

We all looked puzzled, and Frank told us

It was all arranged, and he was real

Tickled we had thought up the idea, and

Jack said we were real imaginative fellahs,

And Frank laughed and said we could

"Bridge the Tombigbee with cocks," and

Bent over and brushed a hair, real or imaginary,

Off one of those grey spats of his,

Saying maybe even Wilson would help us

Make the Dixie Overland Highway safe for

The model A, or something like that; when
Earl told me later he had seen Frank talking
To Buck Oliver, down at the station, saying how
They were snickering like gears in oil,
I was ashamed at what Washington would hear.

Well, he damned well did it. I was down
At the mercantile waiting for Jenny to pick
Out more yarn when Thorn Blount tells
Me Oliver's got some admiral and the
Damn Secretary of the Navy, a Josephus
Daniels talking the President into the idea.
I figured Wilson to be a pretty sharp
Joe, but then Blount says Lloyd George,
Clemenseau, and that Eye-talian Orlando
Were sending roosters back from the
Versailles Conference on the *U.S.S. Northern*
Pacific or some such, and I knew a
Tall tale when it was told.

But, you know, the craziest damned ideas...
I remember picking a cicada shell off a
Hickory branch and wondering what in ...
What had been going on while scientists
Say that thing's been eating roots down
Underground, wondering about the war

Just gone, the war of the whole world,

And not seeing much surprise in it all,

Not after that August auction, the flutter

And squawks of restless birds, beating feathers,

Whipping wings, neck hackles swollen and shining

With the green of flies' bodies, others porcelain

White or oyster-shell blue, the Rhode Island Reds,

Leghorns, and Dominicans, their combs as red and

Fresh as cut flesh, eyes bright as beads,

The smell of dust and cracked corn and that

Wet feather smell amid the grainy smears

On weathered wood—God, but it was pure

Persuasion when all six hundred roosters

And that one pea-eyed hen Helen Keller

Sent in, were by damned sold for more than

Two hundred thousand dollars, as if a

Lifetime sum for a good many folks

Around here could just be spent in fun.

What of poison gas, or cicadas, or giant

Battleships? We had barbequed ribs

And black-eyed peas and biscuits and

Peppery stewed corn, and peach cobbler

And a bridge built by chickens and grins

And a horse-trading heart before you

Were born. See that one-eyed Rhode Island

Red scratching over by the hog pen?

Well, there, and that there is down the line

From Governor Kilby's cock, there's

Where it all began.

On Seeing a Snakeskin Shed in Hurd Cemetery

Sitting at evening, scanning the Times,

You rub heel against calf and feel the skin

Break loose; you reach later for a can of

Beans on a shelf and sense the slide of muscle

Free, by itself, beneath. You pause to scratch

Your back against the wall, and a patch of

Skin, palm-size, pulls free of the ribs,

And you know it's time—to be alone, and

Safe, and private, and born.

You take a personal day from work and tell your

Friends you're out of town, and lock your

Doors and draw down the shades—

Things should be just so, you see, because

It's pride, like peeling an apple, working it off

Whole, no hands. You kick your shoes off

And see the toes clear already, and you squirm them,

All new and clean, in the cool lime carpet,

And leave your clothes in a heap, and you work

Your legs out over the arm of the blue wing-back,

And you roll and curl over the corner of the couch,

Pulling your abdomen loose, and your arms work

And twist free, the skin soft-fuzzed like a ripe peach,

The fingers wriggling, flexing, touching for the first time;

And you contract in back of the coffee-table,

And pump twice, and pull chest and neck free,

Your head working out, as out of some tight

Rubber Halloween mask, the eyes last,

The lens covers pulling off with a soft pock

Sound, and you see with the eyes of a child.

You roll over, lick your lips, and

Curl them into a tiny snake smile.

A Memory Among the Islands

"You remember Alligator Creek?"

"Yeah," I said, my tone wistful, sad, regretful, focused on my father, feeling again Daddy getting into the aluminum runabout tied up to the stern of the houseboat his carpenter foreman had made powered with a paddle-wheel turned by an old Mercury V-8 car engine, I at eleven claiming a seat up near the bow, Lee (Mr. Simes to me, though I avoided that since to say that would be to admit I was not equal) taking the outboard throttle, and we growled across the open water in the dawn, between the tightly-knit mangrove islands that formed the border between the Everglades and the Gulf of Mexico, an area called the Ten Thousand Islands, all looking alike, over fourteen thousand of them in two hundred square miles, a span of twisted roots and waxy green leaves where people sometimes were lost for weeks, though Lee knew where we were, as the prow fell to an idle and nudged amongst the foliage into a winding waterway no more then twenty feet at its widest, and we burbled along, trolling number two Reflecto spoons through the green water and over roots, looking up at wild orchids and air plants, hearing swamp hens, and my father said, "nothing in here but a couple of sunnies," just a moment before the first strike, a snook, bold, leaping, and shining, the black lateral stripe as on some sleek new car, delicately yellowed fins, and I reeled him in and we measured him, Lee saying, "Seventeen inches, eighteen's the limit," and we threw him back, my choked resentment barely dried before the second strike, heavier this time, and I worked at the Penn reel (five lawn jobs' worth) and stiff bay rod, the drag still slipping, until the next one came in, roiling the water, leaping, shaking, open-mouthed, and Lee gaffed him in, unmeasured, an easy two feet, and trolled on for more.

"Yeah," I said. "I remember."

Islamorada

We came down from Miami
With stern parents, borrowed their car,
And set out for adventure, my sister,
Vicki, her friend, and I, two years
Younger at fourteen, and we bought somehow
Cigarettes and Busch beer, and drove out
Across the crushed coral dredged up into
Canaled developments for the amusement
Of our elders, drove out past the planted
Oleanders and braced and fragile key palms,
And parked on the Gulfstream side, the
Ocean side, and listened to "Louie, Louie,"
Accompanied by the wash of the waves—
I can taste it all to this day:
The cool, strong pull of mint and nicotine
In the Newports, the sweaty, yeasty bite
Of the beer, the moan of the wind
Murmuring to our busy pink ears,
Murmuring into the faces of children
So sweetly rejoicing the wicked ways
Of this world, murmuring with a breath
Of wormed timbers and the surgical rubber
Of sargasso weed, of flotsamed fish
And the wealth and birth of what we were

And will be, but we had no time nor need

To listen....

I can hear and taste and feel it

To this day, the tug and touch

Of breeze and waves, of stars and sea

Laving us clean as cherubs dancing

On the shore—

I can feel it to this day,

But could not then.

On Shaving

St. Joseph Peninsula, Florida

As sometimes happens when parents
Part ways, Daniel has become all too often
My summer son and sometime weekend guest
The remainder of the year. And at thirteen known
To his friends as Moe, the Simpsons' cynical barkeep
But in their passioned view at least world weary enough,
He came camping with me, my wife, and toddler child.

And in the late morning hours when teens arise
I, too, tardy this day at the state park shower house
For ablutions stood at the sinks, the concrete floor
Gritty with sand and the beaded salt-laden moisture
That eats through faucets and pipes in three-years
Time—and momentarily the mosquitoes and sand flies
Were at bay outside. On such torpid days I relished an
Old badger brush and tube shave cream after a wash,
Lifting razor to cheek, the silence then broken from two
Sinks away as my son said to me, "Dad, will you
Show me how to shave?" And pleased as I was then,
The mirror blurred with the moment's weight—and
Man and son stepped forward in the steam and I spoke
And we shaved and then packed our gear, pressing
Through the dimpled sand, through spiked palmetto

And stunted live oak, over thorned creeper and pine
Needle mats back to our tents and cold coffee.

I wondered what next we would share, what pass down,
And what I had already missed, in absence
From my sometime son.

Mio-Qua-Coo-Na-Caw (Red Pole)

Principal Village Chief, Shawnee Nation

Died at Pittsburgh, 28 January, 1797

"Lamented by the United States,"

his burial marker says, tight up against

the north wall of Trinity Episcopal Cathedral,

amongst tumbled and tilted stones in a tiny

smear of leaf-green grass between that and

First Presbyterian of Pittsburgh, Sixth

and Smithfield, on a cold and clear November

day two hundred years later, and I thought

about old Red Pole down under there

in a crushed and squeezed plot of ground,

squeezed from the sides by the mountainous

weight of office buildings, department stores,

Kaufman's and Saks and Mutual Life, and squeezed

from below, too, by all the bones of friend

and foe, if such things matter, from Fort Pitt

not far and Fort Duquesne and the burial mound

of the earlier people more his own, and now

the new burial mounds all around and pushing in,

and all the cathedrals, all the cathedrals

raised to praise what one is.

Cathedral after cathedral old Red Pole has seen

rise, the old ones of simple earth dissolving

in the snow, the newer ones of stone or steel,
of prayers and creeds all. Oh, does our
foolishness never end, old man?
"No," he says. "No."

The Fourth Sunday of Easter

"Came Christ the tiger," the panther,

Terrifying, unsought, padding after me,

Breathing, stalking, patient as the still air

In the forest, hot and thick as a jungle day,

Coming after me, growling, a rumbling deep

And smooth as waves rolling over hidden stones,

A growling so a part of the beast it is

An orchestra in the air, soothing and

Drawing me on and back and in—

Came Christ the panther

as smooth and strong and graceful,

As absolutely dangerous

As the beating of my heart—

Oh, God, do not see me here,

Hidden among the leaves—

I am too afraid to be found.

Moncrief Radiation Center

Tattooed

Blue dots like some Maori chief,

Four cornered, and the garish dye

An infected red-violet hue

Brushed on the skull or hip

With a magic mascara wand

In hieroglyphic circles and oblique lines

Intersecting behind ear and eye

Or beneath that umbilical trace -

Hairless heads, innocent blinking eyes

Rolling lashless and afraid, some accepting,

Reading Good Housekeeping, as if

Planning a kitchen were next on the list.

All waiting, all marked and painted supplicants,

For the altar, the invisible touch of prayer,

Measured in millirads and minutes

And a shrinking blot on a backlighted screen.

And the murmuring, the smiles,

The understanding hands while they probe

And nod, the unwept and unweeping,

All the counselors and nurses and friends

Are unwilling to say unhushed

That this is by God cancer,

And this is by God the departure lounge,

And those rads will kill that cancer

Or you, or the cancer you, or your body you,

Or this world you - you are coming

Mighty mighty close to gone - by God.

But you wait, looking over Time Magazine

From fourteen months past,

But what of that, or this, or then?

"Don't scrub the dye off when you wash."

Why wash? Why not just smell to high heaven?

My vision blurs, my ears ring

With radiation and the sea.

"Those conditions will probably pass."

Probably one foot in front of another?

Probably the sun will come up?

Probably my eyes are brown?

Hold me, world.

I'm falling.

And I Had Not

Route 71

Outside Lott, Texas

Their garden sheds and storage buildings,
And two henhouses, what we had been looking
For, well-built, windowed, nesting boxes easy
To access, neat as dolls' houses, lined up along
Texas Route 71, and behind sat a sheet metal barn,
No doors open this Saturday, the farmhouse set back
Further in some oaks, a manicured yard, but I found
No one to chat prices with, and went up to the screen
Door, when out came an elderly suspendered man,
With that moustache-less beard, Mennonite or Quaker
Or Shaker or one of those, telling me his son made
The sheds, didn't know where the son was, maybe in
The barn, and then a young woman appeared, the
Elder going back inside with obvious relief, ceasing
His contact with me.

And she was clad as they are, tight white starched cap,
Gingham dress, brown oxford shoes, white socks, she,
Telling me the prices of the two models, but, no, they
Did not go to Fort Worth.

And as she spoke these disappointing words
And I praised the workmanship of the henhouses,

Their perfect match with what we sought, hoping

I must admit there would be some exception, some

Special dispensation for delivery, I came to realize

How rapt I had become as her clean plain hands were

Still at her sides, her ginger hair pulled back from

A face and eyes bereft of cosmetic metastisis, a

Thin constellation of youth's blemishes across her

Cheeks, but her eyes, the blue of deep sea, bored

Frankly, without guile, into my own—it seemed

Unblinking she looked into my face, through my

Eyes, and offered herself to another person, no

Fear or suspicion, and through her eyes her face

A single lamp, she shone upon me as a surgeon's

Spot, exposing, terrifying me, with what she was,

And I had not.

A Moneychanger Outside The Temple,

Northern Jordan

Below the broken teeth of the Yarmouk hills,

On Irbid's winding streets, in shops and stands,

Arabs mouth, gesticulate the business of the day,

As with Mahmood Hassouneh, one of the eight

Old moneychangers down on Ajloon Street;

A Brit said Mahmood gave reasonable rates,

So in I strode to the dark stone shop,

Half built of blocks chiseled square when

The Romans sought to curb the desert's will,

A teller's cage, a desk, a framed Koranic prayer,

And a green chalkboard scripted in exchange rates;

I spoke slowly to the bespectacled clerk,

And Mahmood swept in from behind a drape,

Like Polonius in an old play or a greying

And grinning Arafat, bowed and took my hand

With rubber-tipped fingers, tacky from soiled currency;

I wanted dinars into dollars, I told him,

A cashier's check on a Stateside bank,

And gave him a thousand dollars' worth,

A roll of bright cash, as he passed me

A scrap of memo pad—"Write your name,"

He said, "and return in two days, maybe three."

The check will be here, he said casually to me,

"Insha'allah," If it is God's will, he said,

And smiled and began to turn away...."But I

Need a...a receipt," I pled in my foreign fear,

Worried and scared as a Christian in a lion's cage....

"Why?" said he, calmly."I will be here each day."

And I had given away a thousand dollars,

Tossed it away - Who would believe it?

And imagining smirks and grins at my back,

I swaggered bravely away.

Returning in three days amidst the alien host,

I waited for the cold laugh, the derisive glare,

As Mahmood directed me to sit and rest;

"But is it here?" I had to know, and he smiled

And said "A moment," and asked if I wanted tea.

Why not? I thought. Can I turn righteous and

Demand what I had no record of? So down I sat,

Commands were shouted, a boy ran for tea,

And we squatted on stools, Mahmood and me,

Looking out on the ebb and flow of market streets,

And we talked of people and towns, as Hassouneh

Took my offered cigarette, disgustedly jutting

A chin at two dusty Egyptian laborers siddling in,

Their greasy rolls of bills spilling out

Onto the plastic counter-top, haggling for

Egyptian pounds, wagging, shouting, pleading

With the clean young clerk behind the bars,

The laborers in striped robes, rubber boots,

Heads wrapped in soil-smeared henna cloths,

Sweeping on into the street, for the mail,

For the cash sent to sick and starving families

Scratching seeds from the sun-baked ruins

Of slums in old Heliopolis or indifferent Cairo.

"Animals," said Mahmood; "They are like beasts,"

And I had heard the the tone before, my mouthcorners

Turned down, disapproving, at what I was not sure;

But we sipped hot mint tea from thin glasses,

Base and rim balanced between finger and thumb,

And sighed and smoked, and saw the shapes and

Sounds and smells of life drift by as in a dream.

And after a slow cigarette's span, the smoke

Whorling up in the still air, just eight minutes

Or so, I rose tentatively, anxiously, to go,

And he handed me a check, slowly stood,

And, hand over heart, he said

"Go in peace," and somehow I did.

On Finding a Grey Fox

Try as I might, and we tried in ways
That only at twelve we can, sometimes
There was, and is, no earning, no reward.
My friend and I scoured trash piles and alleys,
Back yards not our own, and abandoned buildings
And some not as abandoned as we convinced
Ourselves they were, and—of course—mowed
Lawns and washed windows and sometimes even
Killed summer flies in the house at two cents each,
Even if on the sly I propped a door open
So in would fly more; I felt especially blessed
When one special windfall, or what seemed one,
came our way, and we rejoiced as only those who
Worship with new hearts in a new world do.

One summer Tuesday as we, tackle boxes and
Spinning rods in hand, clattered back from fishing
For barracudas we compared to rainbow trout and
Bonefish caught on expeditions for *Field and Stream,*
With dreams of being more than what we were,
Jack and I wound through a plot of tropic green,
A pocket of an earlier time still clutched in the
Midst of a modern Florida, a preserve of banyan,
Ficus and gumbo limbo, causarina and strangler fig,

Of Brazilian pepper and buttonwood, mangrove
And cypress, trimmed with crab-pocked mudbanks
And a chain-link fence. Crossing a clearing we
Caught a movement in the grass, and running
As we did after rabbits or rats, turtles or
Grass snakes, I strode to the spot and saw
On his side in the bright midday sun, unmoving
A grey fox, almost grown, his tongue like
A strip of ham unrolling on one gaped side
Of a toothy jaw, the eyes dull as seeds,
His fur matted over the stark acordian ribs
Slowly moving in and out as if with some
Unheard dirge. And so I claimed him, dead
Or alive, as boys know the value of found
Goods do, and we crept closer, ready to
Run, no fools we, knowing of rattlesnakes
And coral snakes, alligators and scorpions
And rabid dogs or squirrels or raccoons,
And even having learned first-hand the
Pinch of an anole or the sudden crimson flow
Caught from a fish's open mouth; so I
Reached my spinning rod forward and gave
That fox a jab or two, and seeing no
Sign, poked him with a wooden landing net
I had a week before found in someone's trash,
And still only a dragging movement of that wild

Head, like someone in deep sleep—so we bent,
Pushed and scooped the fox into the net and
Strode proudly home, the bounty of the hunt
Over my shoulder....

I built a pen from surplus bricks and, after
A call to Grady Gardner, a friend with pet raccoons,
Force-fed the fox mashed bananas and hamburger meat,
And water dripped down his resisting throat. For
Two weeks I worked at Jason's health (for so
I named him, wandering hero he became to me,
Though later I found him to be female), until
Fur filled out, a nose bright black and wet, and
Pupils tightened in yellow eyes shining with
A wild world that confused my beating heart.

And some two weeks on, after an hour's
June squall, I stepped behind the coral
Garden where his pen leaned, pulled off
The giant washtub that sheltered Jason from
The rain, and bent low to rub those ears
That heard what I could not, and—*click*—
The snap of bright teeth, as back I snatched
My hand, surprised, and said "hey, look,
it's me," and down I reached my hand, and
Click went the teeth, and I urged, angry,

"you're my friend, remember? I saved your

life!" and the dreams of my past weeks fled,

Disney dreams, movie dreams of bears caught

And healed and tamed, wolves loved, trained,

Wild and fearful creatures following their

Child-master-friends to school or into dark

Woods, going for help or saving luckless boys

After a misplaced step led to trapped legs

Or a mineshaft fall, all the dreams I had

Of having and being what others were not

But wished for....and down went my hand,

And again his jaws snapped, and I ground

Between teeth, "You *owe* me!" and wanted so

To stomp that wild ungrateful and resisting

Thing right into the soft earth

But was afraid....

Mother said to me he's not yours and he

Will never be. He's wild and belongs only

To himself--and to the woods, she added.

You'll have to let him go, she said,

And so we did, out into the Everglades,

Then the only wildness left, and I felt

Loss and waste, and understood not a thing,

Not the joy in Oppie's face after letting a

Sparrow go on *The Andy Griffith Show*, nor

The wild desire I know now in seeing a buck

Clear a rancher's fence in a lazy bound

Nor the smug pleasure I feel when a coyote

Looks at me in hatred and disdain, refusing

To be tamed. I could only love then what was

Owned, and yearn now for what would

Not be.

In the Parish Churchyard,

Westbury-on-Trym,

During a New Year

"Here lieth the body of
Scipio Africanus, Negro servant to ye
Right Honourable Charles William
Earl of Suffolk and Bradon
Who died ye 21st December
1720 aged 18 years"
"I who was born a pagan and a slave
Now sweetly sleep a Christian in my grave."

And I know only a fortnight has passed since
Last your eyes, large and luminous as
Flame-reflected gold, closed on our world,
Your arms and fingers, umber smooth and brown,
Finally still, dry, but I still envision your
Sudden grin, the teeth flashing bright and clean,
The instant bloom of white, as if a rose could
Unfold in a blink and close tight the next,
That grin when in we brought that blue satin
Livery, the breeches and stockings around your
Legs, hardly legs but saplings, impossibly slender
Oh, Scipio, I still recall when first old John
Came to the music room, engrossed I was in

Some Venetian's fingering of the new harpsichord,

Come in to tell me the kitchen girls had found

A tiny and trembling boy in the garden, naked as a

Plucked goose and quivering to shake his

Bones apart - you were eight or ten then, we

Never knew, had made your way up from

Bristol Harbour - how you must have darted,

Terrified and lost, between the hooves and carriage

Wheels, past the dogs barking and chasing, out past

Clifton to north of Westbury Village, into my garden.

And after Abigail opened her heart and could not

Lock you up as we had ought, the servants moving

The news through the parishes swift as a fire,

Captain Abraham Jones came calling for you;

Rough he was, with that cold grey eye, grey as a

Well-worked blade, and said you needed a taste

Of the lash, you did, and you'd not be troubling

Good gentlemen such as myself; Oh, I recall

The sneer of contempt crawling to his lip when

I offered ten pounds for you. Twenty, he said,

And took the coins and paced away on his deadly

Business, the tapping of his stick on the paving

Stones ringing out, sounding for all the world

Like the machinery of some infernal clock.

The stones for head and foot are almost finished now,

The color of the clotted cream you loved so much,

And they are African cherubs carved to sing of

Your rest round tablets dark as a raven's wing.

John has planted roses at your feet as

Incarnadine as the blood we shed when

The shards of that crystal vase you dropped

Streaked both our legs with red—and how

You leapt to my calf, linen in hand, to

Staunch the flow with such a cry of

Pain and eye of charity I felt Christ move

Among us like a smoke....

This earth is too large for some, for some too small.

When you chased Charlotte's spaniel on the turf

That day, and returned so blue-lipped from the chill,

I knew too deeply you had stayed too long.

So rest, sweet Scipio, rest your spirit here,

So far from your first home,

So near to the next.

Glouchester Cathedral

Cold thick stones, the floor still

Flecked with rushes, as if no mere

Thousand years had penetrated here,

The hard faces of tombs, of those lying

On their cases, chrysalises of marble

Facing upward, prepared even now to

Rise; and the walls, draped with once-

Crimsoned and azured banners now sere

As cobwebs, paintings dim as old sins

With the smoke from candles, the resin

Of incense, the residue of souls sweating

And rubbing and crying out and up for

Cleansing and hope and care, the souls

Of centuries thick in the air about me

In a supplication so self-sacrificial

As to impoverish the works of my hands,

The walls hold me as once my mother had,

When I had done wrong and knew, and

Knew there was still time to change.

On the Point

Plantation Key, Florida

Out on the Point,

Living in a world of opals, it was:

At sunset when the turquoise bay met

Grey, slick land and was set afire

By the broad watercolor stroke

Of deep conch-colored clouds

Gilded on their swells before

Streaming out into a rose-ribbed

Reflection of the sandbar underfoot.

And I hunkered among drifted buttonwood,

Taking long, harsh pulls of a cupped cigarette,

Watching my mother out on the spit of sand, in

Round-crown Panama and Bermuda shorts, standing

With the stiff rod jutting out level with

The burnishing rim of sky, measuring peace

In yards of braided line, in cut mullet, in

Kinked wire leaders and the oily smell of Off.

And we talked of nothing, nothing I remember,

Words so superfluous with all the world

Speaking at our feet in cries of capped terns

And the silent sermon of an eagle unmoving

On a post marking deep water, clear passage,

Clutching the wood as surely

As we clutched the sand.